Colette

Le Blé en herbe

Jean Duffy

Lecturer in French,
University of Sheffield.

UNIVERSITY OF GLASGOW FRENCH AND GERMAN PUBLICATIONS

1988

University of Glasgow French and German Publications

Series Editors: Mark G. Ward (German)
Geoff Woollen (French)

Consultant Editors : Colin Smethurst
Kenneth Varty

Modern Languages Building, University of Glasgow,
Glasgow G12 8QL, Scotland.

First published 1988.
Reprinted, with minor corrections, 1990.

Printed by Glasgow University Printing Department.

ISBN   0 85261 260 5

Contents

Page references in the text are to the Flammarion edition, with a preface and notes by Claude Pichois (Paris: Garnier-Flammarion, n° 218, 1969).

Introduction

In the course of an interview recorded in *Les Nouvelles Littéraires* in 1926, Colette provided a commentary on *Le Blé en herbe* which at once highlights one of the central thematic threads of the novel and suggests—by means of a theatrical analogy—the reaction which she intended to produce in her reader:

> Le rideau se lève, la scène est plongée dans l'obscurité, deux personnages invisibles dissertent sur l'amour avec beaucoup de science et d'expérience. Lorsqu'à la fin la lumière se fait, les spectateurs surpris s'aperçoivent que les partenaires ont réciproquement quinze et seize ans. Je voulais signifier par là que l'amour passion n'a pas d'âge, et que l'amour n'a pas deux espèces de langage. [...] Je n'ai pas dit autre chose dans *Le Blé en herbe*. J'ai seulement intercalé dans ce récit quelques paysages cancalais qui m'avaient vivement émue. [1]

Colette's remarks act as a corrective to the unwary reader who might be too readily tempted to dismiss *Le Blé en herbe* as a straightforward account of adolescent love. While it is true that the book is adolescent fiction insofar as it offers an acutely-observed analysis of teenage development centred on the specific relationship between its two protagonists, its implications extend far beyond the particular couple and the particular relationship. Many of its themes are those of Colette's work as a whole, and its analysis of the relationship between Vinca and Phil is applicable to the relationship between men and women in general.

Ironically, it was precisely this dimension of the work which generated publication problems for its author. If Colette wished to surprise her readers and to challenge their preconceptions about adolescence and love, tactically she should not have begun by shocking her publisher. Published in book form in 1923, *Le Blé en herbe* was originally conceived as a serial for *Le Matin,* to which Colette was a regular contributor. Once it became apparent that Colette planned a sexual consummation of the relationship between Vinca and Phil, publication of the serial was suspended, a decision which partly explains the discrepancy between the very brief first fifteen chapters and the long, antepenultimate chapter. The seduction of the young man by the older woman was acceptable in terms of the conventions of the time because it preserved the illusion of innocence; the willing participation of a young girl in sexual intercourse with one of her peers—even though it was essential to Colette's logic of passion—constituted too much of a challenge to the paternalistic morality of the day.

To the extent that it clarifies her intentions and inhibits facile literary or moral judgments, Colette's comment on *Le Blé en herbe* constitutes a useful interpretive key to the novel. What it fails to do, however, is to give an indication of the thematic richness and technical complexity of the text. In giving prominence to what is undoubtedly the central issue of *Le Blé en herbe* —'l'amour passion'—Colette has underplayed the other thematic threads running through the text and the relationships which she establishes between them. Even more misleading is her summary statement on approach, dismissing it as a combination of *récit* and natural description, which fails drastically to do justice both to the problems which she must have encountered in unifying a work which was initially conceived as a feuilleton, and to those facing any mature writer who chooses to recreate the perceptual world of an adolescent protagonist.

NOTES

(1)   Frédéric Lefèvre, 'Une Heure avec Colette', *Les Nouvelles Littéraires,* 27 March 1926.

Chapter One

Structure and Motif

Structure

The most cursory perusal of Colette's collected work reveals her as both a highly productive writer and an extremely economical artist. Over a literary career spanning half a century, she published novels, plays, several volumes of memoirs and innumerable essays, articles and reviews. If Colette was prolific, however, she was rarely verbose. Her individual works are almost invariably brief, many of them closer in form to the *nouvelle* or the Gidean *récit* than to the convoluted novel that had been developed by the previous generation. To some extent this brevity and relative simplicity is to be attributed to publication conditions. The great majority of her novels were the result of commissions; a substantial number of them were written for serialisation in reviews and literary magazines. The same publication conditions also determined in some measure the internal divisions of the individual works. Space restrictions and editorial deadlines precluded long, heavily-worked chapters. An examination of the first fifteen chapters of *Le Blé en herbe* shows very clearly the way in which Colette moulded her craft and composition to suit the demands of serialisation.

The manuscript of *Le Blé en herbe* reveals that the work was originally conceived as a series of *contes,* each headed by a title which was suppressed in the final version: 'La Crevette'; 'Vinca'; 'En attendant'; 'Daphnis'; 'Drames'; 'Sérénité'; 'Les Ombres'; 'L'Antre'; 'Les Chardons'; 'La Soumission'; 'Nocturne'; 'Faiblesse'; 'Pardon'; 'La Quémandeuse'; 'La Comparaison'.[1] The serial format made considerable demands on the discipline and compositional skills of the writer, who had to provide an

3

episode which was not only complete and satisfying in itself but also a component in a continuous narrative to be followed perhaps more than a month later in a subsequent edition of *Le Matin*. The effects of these apparently contradictory demands can be readily seen in the composition of *Le Blé en herbe*. The progress of the narrative centres upon a number of critical incidents which have important reverberations on the level of the characters' emotions—for example, Phil's chance encounters with Madame Dalleray on the dunes and at the gate of *Ker-anna*—or which are in fact the result of those emotions—for example, Phil's seduction by Madame Dalleray, his highly charged reaction to what he perceives as Vinca's cruelty to other creatures, his syncope on his walk with his father. These dramatic incidents punctuate the otherwise uneventful narrative and provide the serial reader with memorable points of reference in his reading of subsequent episodes. It is in these chapters and in the paradoxical, dramatic or unfinished sentences which conclude many of her chapters that Colette makes most concessions to the serial. While the unfinished sentence often leaves room for fruitful readerly speculation, its abuse makes it something of an irritating tic in *Le Blé en herbe*.

More often than not, however, Colette managed to turn the restrictions of the serial to her advantage. In this novel where incisiveness is at a premium, the telling moment has precedence over continuity and consequentiality. The first fifteen chapters of the novel record discrete moments in the course of this momentous summer in Brittany which wreaks so many changes in the relationship between Phil and Vinca and in his relationship with his body, his past and his social group. The panoramic summaries which novelists use so freely to bring the reader up to date on events preceding major scenes and the "filler" phrases ('le lendemain...'; 'deux jours plus tard...', etc.), which offer temporal points of reference and maintain a sense of continuity, are absent from *Le Blé en herbe*. In each chapter the characters are presented *in medias res,* engaged in some activity or conversation:

—Tu vas à la pêche, Vinca ? (p. 31)

Ils nageaient côte à côte... (p. 37)

Il essaya de la prière... (p. 57)

Au tournant de la petite route, Phil sauta à terre... (p. 79)

Such indications of time as are given are offered by the characters themselves in their desultory conversations, and rarely establish a clear connection with events of the preceding chapter:

—Les vacances, à présent, c'est l'affaire d'un mois et demi, quoi! (p. 43)

—C'est incroyable ce que les jours raccourcissent! (p. 72)

—Il est fixé, le jour de votre départ pour Paris? demanda Madame Dalleray. (p. 122)

Colette's exposition is minimal: immediacy is essential to the format she has chosen and where possible she will show rather than tell. Even in the opening chapter, she opts to present her characters in situation rather than to provide the reader with a potted background history. Her opening paragraph introduces Vinca in mid-gesture and establishes crucial facts about her appearance and personality by reference to Phil's view of her and through the subconversation which underlies all of her and Phil's communication with each other, rather than by a disruptively conspicuous narratorial summary:

—Tu vas à la pêche, Vinca?
D'un signe de tête hautain, la Pervenche, Vinca aux yeux couleur de pluie printanière, répondit qu'elle allait, en effet, à la pêche. Son chandail reprisé en témoignait et ses espadrilles racornies par le sel. On savait que sa jupe à carreaux bleus et verts, qui datait de trois ans et laissait voir ses genoux, appartenait à la crevette et aux crabes. Et ces deux havenets sur l'épaule, et ce béret de laine hérissé et bleuâtre comme un chardon des dunes, constituaient-ils une panoplie de pêche, oui ou non? (p. 31)

Colette begins her story with a moment which is typical of the history of the characters and speaks volumes about their relationship with each other, in particular their familiarity and their intuitive communication; a narratorial intrusion would render neither so satisfactorily or so immediately.

5

The relationship between the adolescent protagonists and their families is likewise encapsulated in a representative moment in the chapter originally entitled 'Les Ombres'. Here, through a mixture of dialogue, play of glances and snatches of thought, Colette reveals with a minimum of explicit commentary the marginal role of their parents in the lives of Phil and Vinca and the amusing contrast between what Vinca and Phil see as the puerility of their parents and their own slightly melodramatic gravity.

If Colette makes the representative moment do the work of the traditional expository commentary, elsewhere in the text she replaces the knowing narratorial prognostication with a symbolic scene or description which prefigures subsequent developments. Thus, in Chapter Five, the alert reader recognises that Phil's attempt to put away the games scattered around the terrace is more than a way of filling a desultory rainy day. His activity and the tear-like raindrops running down the windowpane separating Vinca from him herald the end of childish pursuits and the entry into a world of passion, in which communication is hampered by transparent but effective barriers:

> Il ramassa sur la terrasse les boules cloutées d'acier et le cochonnet de buis, abandonnés le matin, les tambourins et les balles de caoutchouc. Il rangea dans une resserre ces jouets qui ne l'amusaient plus, comme on range les pièces d'un déguisement qui doit servir longtemps. Derrière la fenêtre les yeux de la Pervenche le suivaient et les gouttes glissantes, le long de la vitre, semblaient ruisseler de ces yeux anxieux... (p. 58)

In the following chapter this omen would at first seem to be belied as time momentarily seems to give them a reprieve. Here, they try to bypass the sexual dimension of the male-female relationship through a picnic *en famille* with Lisette which is a return to the childish imitation of the adult world. However, in their recreation of a childish illusion they have failed to take account of the inexorable drive of the subconscious. The symbolism of Phil's dream which concludes the chapter may be less direct than that of the previous chapter, but its sexual connotations are unmistakable:

> Son rêve viril où l'amour, devançant l'âge de l'amour, se
> laissait lui-même distancer par ses fins généreuses et simples,
> fonça vers des solitudes dont il fut le maître. Il dépassa une
> grotte,—un hamac de fibres creusé sous une forme nue, un feu
> rougeoyant qui battait de l'aile à ras de terre—puis perdit son
> sens divinatoire, sa puissance de vol, chavira, et toucha le fond
> moelleux du plus noir repos. (p. 71)

Indeed, the sexual implications of this passage are confirmed and
corroborated by a reprise of its vocabulary in the passage evoking Phil's
submission to Madame Dalleray:

> Il baissa la tête, vit passer devant lui deux ou trois images
> incohérentes, inéluctables, de vol comme l'on vole en songe, de
> chute comme l'on choit en plongeant... (pp. 99-100)

These two passages are in fact stages in the development of a sustained
image relating to flight and fall which is initiated by the reference to the
flight of curlews observed by Phil (p. 39). At this early point in the text, the
reader is tempted to interpret the reference as a symbolic omen of the union
of the two young, wild creatures, Phil and Vinca. A second allusion is made
to a pair of curlews, however, immediately after Phil's sexual initiation by
Madame Dalleray, and acts as a cruel and ironic reminder of the carefree
world which he believes he has lost:

> Un couple de courlis passa au-dessus de Philippe assez bas
> pour qu'il entendît le cri de voilure de leurs ailes tendues, et leur
> piaulement sur la mer plongea, dans la mémoire ouverte et sans
> défense de l'adolescent, jusqu'au fond de quinze années
> pures... (p. 105)

Through the elaboration of a series of related symbolic moments, Colette
has been able to convey both the subconscious sexual connotations of Phil's
relationship with Vinca and the rather melodramatic implications which he
consciously chooses to draw from his relationship with Madame Dalleray.

Of the symbolic moments of the novel, it is, however, the picking of the
'chardons bleus' which is the most significant. In his choice as a gift for
Madame Dalleray of flowers which throughout his childhood he has
associated with Vinca, Phil is committing an act of treachery which will
adulterate his relationship both with Vinca and Madame Dalleray:

7

> Mais un creux de dune entre la villa et la mer, empli jusqu'aux
> bords de chardons des sables, bleus dans leur fleur, mauves au
> long de leur tige cassante, méritait de s'appeler 'le miroir des
> yeux de Vinca'. (p. 89)

The unwary reader will too readily attribute this gesture to adolescent thoughtlessness and clumsiness. For it will be on the same issue that Vinca will challenge him in her confrontation with him in the sixteenth chapter, i.e. that he has given to Madame Dalleray what belonged to Vinca, whether that be his virginity or a symbolic bunch of wild flowers (p. 170). Furthermore, in his enthusiasm, Phil fails to pay due respect to the dangers of his adventure—his laceration of his hands on the barbs of the thistles acts as a warning that he will not emerge unscathed: 'Il coupa et bottela secrètement les plus beaux chardons, en se blessant furieusement les mains à leur feuillage de fer' (p. 89).

That Colette overcame the problems posed by serial publication is, then, borne out by the relatively few concessions which she made to her readership in the first fifteen chapters, demanding a high level of literary competence and an alertness to the potential significance of the apparently innocuous detail. A question mark remains, however, over the balance and coherence of the finished work. Most critics see the discrepancy between the first fifteen chapters and the very long antepenultimate chapter as an imbalance to be explained by the lifting of constraints after the suspension of serial publication. Considered in this light alone, the artistic integrity of the work is profoundly challenged. What this view fails to acknowledge, however, is the fundamental fact that there was no over-riding practical reason why Colette did not choose to continue *Le Blé en herbe* in the manner in which she had started it. That she changed her tactics was clearly an aesthetic choice and, in my opinion, a choice which was determined by the logic of her narrative. A comparison between the earlier part of the novel and the long sixteenth chapter reveals more than a difference in length; it also reveals a change in tempo and a highly important shift in focus.

In the first fifteen chapters of the novel, the development of Phil's sexual awareness and libido is charted principally through his relationship with Madame Dalleray. Throughout these first fifteen chapters he is able to compartmentalise in his own mind the conflicting demands of his situation—on the one hand, childhood, Vinca and reassuring and respectable family life; on the other, adulthood, Madame Dalleray and the alarming world of illicit love. Phil's compartmentalisation of his life begins with his first encounter with Madame Dalleray on the dunes. In this scene—the only one in the novel where Vinca and Madame Dalleray actually see one another—the immediate mutual suspicion shown by the two female characters places Phil in an apparent position of control and hints at a choice which is totally new to him. His reaction to Vinca's surprise at Madame Dalleray's hasty departure shows a certain pleasure in generating mystery and an ambivalence which, in the course of the work, will develop into deceit and doublethink.

> —Et pourquoi est-ce qu'elle est partie si vite, juste au moment où je venais ?
> Philippe prit son temps avant de répondre. Il goûta de nouveau, en secret, l'assurance sans gestes, le ferme regard de l'inconnue, et son sourire méditatif. Il se souvint qu'elle l'appelait 'Monsieur' gravement. Mais il se souvint aussi qu'elle avait dit 'Vinca' tout court, d'une manière trop familière et un peu injurieuse. Il fronça les sourcils et son regard protégea l'innocent désordre de son amie. Il rêva un moment et trouva une réponse ambiguë qui satisfaisait en même temps son goût de secret romanesque et sa pudibonderie de jeune bourgeois.
> —Elle a aussi bien fait, répondit-il. (pp. 55-6)

In the course of the first part of the novel, he successfully—or so he thinks—conducts his relationship in a way which protects the innocence of his friend and preserves the integrity of his childhood. His first visit to Madame Dalleray's house divides his world into reality and dream, the familiar and the exotic:

> La vie de Philippe appartenait toujours à Vinca, à la petite amie de son cœur, née tout près de lui, douze mois après lui, attachée à lui comme une jumelle à son frère jumeau, anxieuse comme une amante qui doit demain perdre son amant. Mais le rêve, ni le cauchemar ne dépendent de la vie réelle. Un mauvais rêve, riche d'ombre glaciale, de rouge sourd, de velours noir et or, empiétait sur la vie de Phil, diminuait, en segment d'éclipse, les heures normales du jour... (pp. 87-8)

By the following chapter, his polarisation of the two parts of his life has become so rigid that Madame Dalleray's polite reference to his family causes him to start in surprise: '"Vos parents vont bien, Monsieur Phil ?" [...] Du bord de sa manche, il accrocha une cuiller, qui tomba avec un son de clochette faible sur le tapis'(p. 99). Phil's ultimate seduction by Madame Dalleray drives, it seems to him, an immovable wedge between the past and the future. The life which hitherto had appeared to be so rich in memories and in potential is suddenly fractured by a single word: the preposition '*avant* ' (p. 139).

In his melodramatic division of his life into two irreconcilable parts and in his obsession with his own development, Philippe has wilfully ignored the changes taking place simultaneously in Vinca: 'le texte de Colette tend à relever que [l'] aspect parfois obtus du caractère masculin n'est pas dû à quelque infériorité de l'homme en face d'une intuition féminine inégalable et innée—mais plutôt le résultat du peu de mal qu'il se donne pour comprendre sa compagne.' [2] Throughout the novel, the reader is made equally aware of the physical changes wrought by puberty in each character. For every reference to the growth of Phil's moustache, there is another to the development of Vinca's feminine charm:

> ... un corps chaque jour féminisé... (p. 110)

> ...ses seins qu'un peu de chair douce, toute neuve, arrondissait. (p. 164)

Phil notes these changes, but refuses to acknowledge Vinca as a sexual and sensual being, both through fear of adulterating his image of childhood and because a sexually aware Vinca challenges his illusion of power over her:

> ...la forme du long corps vigoureux de son amie—corps familier, pourvu chaque année de beautés nouvelles et prévues—lui apparut pour le frapper de stupeur.
> Qu'y avait-il de commun entre ce corps, entre l'emploi que l'amour en pouvait faire, entre ses fins inévitables, et la destinée d'un autre corps de femme, voué à des rapts délicats, doué d'un génie spoliateur, d'une implacabilité passionnée, d'une enchanteresse et hypocrite pédagogie? (p. 106)

Furthermore, throughout the first part of the book he has confused virginity with innocence and has failed to recognise the development of womanly intuition in Vinca, whose suspicions were aroused as early as Chapter Ten:

> Mais la pureté vigilante de Vinca percevait, par des avertissements soudains, une présence féminine auprès de Philippe. Il arrivait qu'elle flairât l'air, autour de lui, comme s'il eût, en secret, fumé, ou mangé une friandise. (p. 96)

It is in the long, antepenultimate chapter that Vinca finally forces Phil to see her as she is, to recognise her awakened libido. In this chapter, the tempo changes dramatically as events start to overtake Phil, and the staccato rhythm established by the earlier short chapters gives way to an inexorable drive towards the conclusion. In this chapter, major crises follow fast and furious: the departure of Madame Dalleray, Vinca's confrontation with Phil, the physical consummation of their relationship which is orchestrated by Vinca rather than by Phil. The simplistic opposition which Phil has created in his own mind between Vinca and Madame Dalleray collapses as he recognises not only the common denominator which unites them—passion—but also their autonomy:

> Elle ferma les yeux, renversa la tête, caressa de la voix ses dernières paroles, et ressembla, avec une fidélité étrange, à toutes les femmes qui renversent le col et ferment les yeux sous un excès de bonheur. Pour la première fois, Phil reconnut en Vinca la sœur de celle qui, les yeux clos et la tête abandonnée, semblait se séparer de lui, dans les instants même où il la tenait le mieux embrassée... (pp. 157-8)

His recognition is a reluctant one and, right to the end of the novel, he tries to preserve his initial position, but Vinca has set in motion an irresistible mechanism which is designed to destroy his attempts to idealise her and deny her reality. Now her slightest gesture is likely to remind him of Madame Dalleray: 'Involontairement il compara à cette vigilance de tous les sens féminins, le souvenir d'une autre habileté féminine' (p. 181). Even in sleep he is not allowed respite from his recent revelation, as Vinca intrudes upon his dreams and adopts the role taken previously by Madame Dalleray:

11

> Ici Camille Dalleray portait le visage de Vinca; là Vinca,
> autoritaire, régnait sur lui avec une froideur impure et
> prestidigitatrice. (p. 175)

As in his earlier seduction, it is the woman who takes the initiative. In the sexual act, the loss of Vinca's virginity is not the issue; it is the loss of Phil's illusions which is the more marking psychological event. Try as he may, in the short epilogue chapter, to salvage the vestiges of those illusions, he cannot but recognise that he has been outwitted by the feminine principle.

That the history and composition of *Le Blé en herbe* pose peculiar problems for the critic is undeniable. But the suggestion that the unusual composition of the novel is to be explained by contingent, extratextual circumstances is to ignore the choices open to Colette and to deny her artistic control of her work. From the foregoing analysis it should be clear that what may initially seem to be an imbalance in the text is in fact the effect of a conscious and deliberate tailoring of the structure of the text to the development of the action and the themes. The sustained staccato rhythm of the first fifteen chapters corresponds to Phil's mental and physical toing and froing between Madame Dalleray and Vinca; the disruption of this rhythm by the sweeping sixteenth chapter translates into formal terms the disruption of Phil's newly-established routine by events and people lying outside his control.

The Motif

The finely-tuned equilibrium which Colette establishes between the demands of serialisation and those of aesthetic unity can also be seen in her use of the motif. In his introduction to the Garnier-Flammarion edition of the text, Claude Pichois draws attention to the repetitions to be found in the novel, attributing them in part to the need to provide *aides-mémoire* for the readers of the serial. Such an interpretation certainly goes some way towards explaining the recurrence of descriptive detail and epithets relating to Phil, Vinca and Madame Dalleray. However, as Pichois is careful to point out, Colette chose not to eliminate such repetition in the final version. In fact, the motif is one of Colette's hallmarks. Broadly speaking, the elaboration of a network of motifs which span the novel not only serves to unify the work but also performs an emphatic function, drawing attention, through repetition, to key ideas and themes. Furthermore, the carefully developed motif may often act as a kind of economical shorthand which, by replacing explicit narratorial analysis or commentary, involves the reader more positively in the interpretation of the text.

Of the many motifs running through *Le Blé en herbe,* the references to colour which punctuate the text illustrate these points most clearly. As Malcolm Offord points out in 'Colours in Colette's *Le Blé en herbe* ':

> Each time a colour occurs, [...] it gives an insight into the emotional states of the major characters and into their attitudes towards each other and themselves. [3]

The mood of the character literally colours his or her perception not only of the present, but also of the past and the future:

> L'adolescent doutait de sa mémoire en ressassant ces images d'un coloris brûlant et faux... (p. 88)

> —Elle a de la chance, de pouvoir penser à la couleur de l'avenir, en ce moment ! (p. 163)

> La zone colorée de ses espoirs ne dépassait pas la fin de la journée... (p. 139)

People too are subject to the process of colour projection. The opposition between Vinca and Madame Dalleray is developed and stylised through the attribution to them of key identifying colours. Phil associates Vinca primarily with blue—the colour of her eyes, many of her clothes, the colour of the sea, the sky and the flowers on the dunes. It is a cipher for her naturalness and her simplicity. Madame Dalleray by contrast is the 'Dame en blanc', the mysterious lady in white who appears in Phil's life only to wreak havoc and as suddenly to disappear. As Offord notes, white is here 'impersonal, lacking in warmth and depth, even verging on the inhuman.' [4] In her choice of attire, Madame Dalleray is clearly contriving to create a very stylised, sophisticated and dramatic image which contrasts sharply with Vinca's haphazard dress. While nature complements Vinca's robust beauty (p. 69), Madame Dalleray resorts to more subtle, artificial effects (p. 90). Furthermore, while Vinca's appearance mirrors that of her environment, Madame Dalleray clearly creates a piquant counterpoint between the white of her clothes—normally the colour of purity—and the sumptuous and assertively colourful décor which she inhabits: '...ses [Phil's] yeux habitués discernèrent le rouge et le blanc d'une tenture, le noir et l'or assourdi des rideaux' (p. 83).

Ultimately more interesting than this contrast is the selectiveness on which it is based. Phil stylises the roles of Madame Dalleray and Vinca by the application of the epithets 'la Dame en blanc' and 'la Pervenche', ignoring the frequency with which Vinca too is dressed in white (pp. 39, 60, 66, 68, 75, 108, 153). Once again the opposition which Phil has set up between the two women in his life is seen to be based on a highly selective view of Vinca. Phil's own inconsistency is highlighted ironically by the reprise of and variation on an analogy used disparagingly to describe Vinca and later, admiringly, to describe Madame Dalleray:

> —Un dimanche à Tahiti, railla Philippe en lui-même. Je ne l'ai jamais vue si laide. (p. 39)

> Enroulé dans une une étoffe ample et blanche comme la robe des femmes de Tahiti... (p. 122)

In his desire to retain his childish image of Vinca in her well-worn clothes, Phil cannot accommodate a new view of her. Blinded by the dazzle and exoticism of Madame Dalleray, he fails to acknowledge the common feminine coquettishness which characterises both women, albeit in different degrees.

*****

While Colette inevitably made certain concessions to the broad audience of *Le Matin,* it is clear from the foregoing discussion that she also required a high degree of literary sophistication and participation on the part of her readers. In particular, she demanded of them an ability to recognise the thematic implications of certain structural choices, an alertness to the layer of the unspoken which underlies her symbolic scenes, and a good textual memory capable of correlating and interpreting recurrent motifs. Far from being a slave to the demands of serialisation, Colette shows in *Le Blé en herbe* the way in which she was able not only to transcend these limits, but also to set her own aesthetic standards.

NOTES

(1)   See Pichois's introduction to the Flammarion edition, pp. 19-20.

(2)   Anne A. Ketchum, *Colette ou la naissance du jour: étude d'un malentendu* (Paris: Minard, 1968), p. 211.

(3)   *Nottingham French Studies*, 22 (1984), 32-53 [pp. 51-2].

(4)   *Ibid.*, p. 45.

Chapter Two

Adolescence in *Le Blé en herbe*

While Colette stresses the universality of her analysis of human relations in *Le Blé en herbe,* it is nevertheless true that she also offers an extremely nuanced analysis of adolescence. The choice of a particular, critical summer in the lives of Vinca and Phil allows her to explore through her protagonists the specific tensions and uncertainty which characterise the transition from childhood to adulthood. Adolescence is an age which is dominated by conflicting demands, ambivalence and confusion. Above all, perhaps, it is a period of change: the adolescent has to accommodate in a relatively short space of time signs of physical development in himself and his peers, shifts in social expectations and mores. Familiar and apparently firm points of reference suddenly, it seems, are undermined by unfamiliar experiences, and he finds that his perception of his world, of his past, present and his future, has to alter accordingly. These changes will be the principal subject of this chapter.

On the most obvious level, the transition from childhood to adulthood manifests itself in physical terms. Although Colette does not dwell on this aspect, as we have already seen, she nevertheless punctuates her narrative with descriptive detail which registers the rapid physical development that characterises adolescence. More interesting ultimately to Colette, however, is the way in which these physical changes affect the protagonists' perception of themselves and each other. This is the awkward age, an indeterminate phase in which adult and childish forms do battle with each other inside the adolescent's body:

> —bras et jambes de seize ans, minces, mais d'une forme pleine d'où le muscle sec n'avait pas encore émergé et qui pouvaient enorgueillir une jeune fille autant qu'un jeune homme. (p. 51)

16

It is also an age in which the individual becomes acutely aware of his or her own body—an awareness capable of generating narcissistic pleasure:

> Phil soupira, atteint d'un bonheur vague et sans tache auquel la fatigue agréable, la vibration de ses muscles encore tendus par l'escalade [...] versaient, chacune, leur part. Il s'assit [...] et revit avec surprise le bronze nouveau de ses jambes, de ses bras... (p. 51)

> Il se savait beau à cette minute, les joues chaudes, la bouche lustrée, le front couché dans un désordre harmonieux de cheveux noirs. (p. 70)

but also of creating inhibitions which are physically unjustified and belied by other childish habits:

> ... et si elle ferme étroitement, sur une gorge absente, blousons et chandails, elle trousse jupe et culotte pour descendre à l'eau, aussi haut qu'elle peut, avec une sérénité de petit garçon... (p. 32)

> Elle parlait d'un air dur et puéril, en tirant machinalement sur sa robe comme si elle eût voulu écraser ses seins. (p. 167)

For some, adolescent indeterminacy confers a fleeting beauty before they are finally assimilated into adult uniformity. Such is the case of Phil:

> Elle [Vinca] contempla, désabusée, les traits qui seraient sans doute, plus tard, ceux d'un homme brun assez banalement agréable, mais que la dix-septième année, pour un peu de temps encore, retenait en deçà de la virilité. (pp. 166-7)

Vinca's charitable silence here is commendable, and contrasts sharply with Phil's earlier cruel attack on her personal appearance:

> —Dieu, que tu es mal peignée, Vinca ! [...]
> —Je sais bien... Je serai mal coiffée tant que mes cheveux seront trop courts. Cette coiffure-là, c'est en attendant.
> —La laideur temporaire, ça t'est égal... (p. 44)

It is highly ironic, of course, that of the two it is Vinca who, despite her temporary flaws, shows most potential for the future. It takes an outsider, the guest of Chapter Two, to make Phil stand back and look at his companion with new eyes:

> —Elle devient ravissante! Ravissante! Dans deux ans... vous
> la verrez !
> Vinca entendit, jeta un vif regard féminin sur l'étranger, et
> sourit. La bouche pourpre se fendit sur une lame de dents
> blanches, les prunelles, bleues comme la fleur dont elle portait
> le nom, se voilèrent de cils blonds, et Phil lui-même fut ébloui.
> (p. 40)

His recognition of her incipient beauty, however, offers Phil no comfort; on the contrary, the stranger's compliment and Vinca's reaction to it reveal to him how tenuous is his control over her.

The appearance of the guest in Chapter Two introduces another problem relating to the transition between childhood and adulthood: that of the behaviour expected of the adolescent who suddenly finds himself having to cope with two quite different codes and sets of expectations. On the one hand, the adults around Vinca and Phil expect them to conform to the rules which have governed their childhood:

> —Eh, eh, déjà dix heures. Les enfants, vous n'avez pas l'air de
> vous douter qu'on se couche à dix heures, ici ? (p. 116)

On the other hand, they demand of them a display of social graces which belong properly to the adult world, and are quick to mock what they see as the residue of childish behaviour:

> —Ah ! quand tu auras l'âge de raison, toi, je ferai une croix à la
> cheminée! (p. 76)

Vinca deals with these conflicting demands rather better than Phil and shows the making of a consummate hostess (p. 40). Phil's confusion and difficulties in adapting to adolescence are conveyed by comparisons, drawn by the narrator, other characters or himself, between his behaviour or appearance and that of a much younger boy (pp. 53, 59, 77, 176).

Phil is, admittedly, faced with a rather more demanding and confusing situation in his relationship with Madame Dalleray. In his dealings with her he is constantly being caught between the bourgeois code governing adult-child relationships and the amorous code, and the progress of his relationship with her is punctuated by faux pas which reflect his uneasiness.

A practised *mondaine,* she is quick in her first encounter with him to turn her own social gaffe to her advantage and takes great pleasure in his discomfiture. Throughout their first meetings she plays expertly on the ambiguities of the situation, shifting back and forth between the two codes:

> —Prenez garde, je vais vous tutoyer: vous paraissez douze ans, quand vous riez.
> Mais elle le regardait dans les yeux, comme un homme. (p. 53)

Phil himself exploits, albeit unconsciously, the same ambiguities to further his amorous ambitions. His decision to give her a bunch of flowers in repayment for the glass of orange she offered him belongs to the code of politeness which his bourgeois background has demanded of him as a child. Ironically, of course, he is using the rules of that code to facilitate a relationship which contravenes that same code: 'Je lui dois une politesse. [...] Il faut que je dépose des fleurs à sa porte...'(p. 89). In playing with two different codes, both Phil and Madame Dalleray are taking considerable risks. Phil, because of his naivety and confusion, manages clumsily to offend rather than to please, and Madame Dalleray treats him as the child he pretended to be rather than the lover he aspired to be:

> —J'ai pensé que ça vous serait agréable... Et puis vous m'aviez offert de l'orangeade...
> —Personne ne vous a demandé à m'être agréable. Quittez donc l'obligeant souci qui vous amène, aujourd'hui, à me bombarder de chardons bleus. (p. 92)

Ultimately, of course, Madame Dalleray's manipulation of the rules of the game backfires on her too. While she is in control, she shifts comfortably back and forth between the two codes, demanding at one moment the subservience of the lover—'Je n'aime que les mendiants et les affamés, Monsieur Phil' (p. 92)—and at others enquiring politely after Phil's parents (pp. 84, 99). So that when she backs Phil into a corner, he may retreat behind the code of family obligation: '"Je ne suis pas un petit vagabond libre. Et je n'ai que seize ans et demi." Elle rougit lentement' (p. 126).

*****

19

Family obligation accounts for another difference between adulthood and childhood in *Le Blé en herbe*. While Vinca and Phil have enjoyed a carefree childhood in which adult preoccupations have had but a marginal influence on their life, adolescence has forced upon them considerations relating to their future which threaten their independence and intimacy. In a number of scenes, Colette draws attention to the very different expectations affecting the sexes. Even as they advocate a patience which is intolerable to the adolescent (p. 47), and feeds his or her feeling of indeterminacy, the adults insist on sketching out quite specific plans for the same adolescent's future. Again and again, through discussions between the protagonists and among their parents and through reference to the various domestic chores undertaken by Vinca, Colette stresses that entry into adulthood brings with it a separation of the roles demanded of the male and female. The female child is expected to acquire domestic and social skills which will ultimately befit a wife and mother, and which in the meantime will contribute to the running of the parental household (p. 48). More far-reaching aspirations, whether it be the continuation of her education or the pursuit of a career, are discouraged, indeed dismissed:

> —Je ne passe pas mon bachot, moi.
> —Tu seras quoi ? Tu te décides, ou non, pour le dessin industriel ? Ou la pharmacie ?
> —Maman a dit [...] qu'elle a des rhumatismes, que Lisette n'a que huit ans, et que sans aller chercher si loin j'ai de quoi m'occuper chez nous, que bientôt je tiendrai les comptes de la maison, je devrai diriger l'éducation de Lisette, les domestiques, tout ça, enfin... [ ] Que je me marierai. (p. 48)

Interestingly, it is the female rather than the male who chooses to maintain the tradition and to preclude automatically other alternatives. Indeed, both Phil and Monsieur Audebert both react quite violently to Vinca's acceptance and her mother's dogmatism on the subject:

> —Et ça te suffit ? Ça te suffit pour... voyons, cinq, six ans, peut-être plus ? (p. 49)

> —Voilà une enfant que tu prétends garder à la maison, bon. Quelle pâture donneras-tu à son activité morale et physique ? (pp. 73-4)

Despite his apparently much greater freedom of choice, Phil finds that the future and the burden of family obligation are beginning to adulterate the pleasure of the present. Adolescence has brought responsibilities which he and Vinca have hitherto been able to leave to other people:

> —Ces années où il faut avoir l'air, devant papa et maman, d'aimer une carrière pour ne pas les désoler... (p. 47)

Moreover, an inventory of the possibilities open to him as a son of the petite bourgeoisie reveals a very limited and limiting range of choices which reduce the glamour of adulthood to a repetition of the lives of the adults he knows:

> —Mon avenir, voyons, mon avenir... C'est bien simple... Si je ne fais pas mon droit, mon avenir, c'est le magasin de papa, glacières pour hôtels, châteaux; phares, pièces détachées et quincaillerie pour l'automobile. Le bachot, et tout de suite après le magasin, les clients, la correspondance... Papa n'y gagne pas de quoi avoir son auto... Ah! il y a aussi mon service militaire... (pp. 138-9)

In her examination of the differentiation between the sexes which accompanies adolescence, Colette is not, then, making a radical feminist statement; rather she is bemoaning the loss of the freedom which characterises childhood and which starts to disappear with the onset of adolescence.

*****

This loss of freedom is accompanied by the beginning of an alienation from the natural world. Phil and Vinca have been and still are to varying degrees 'enfants sauvages'. Their entire childhood is inextricably bound up with their natural environment, in particular with the Breton landscape in which they have passed their vacations:

> Mais quand il disait dans son cœur: 'Vinca!', le nom appelait, inséparable de son amie, le souvenir du sable, chaud aux genoux, serré et fuyant au creux des paumes... (p. 75)

Their knowledge of their environment and its inhabitants is intimate:

> Philippe connaissait la côte par cœur, depuis qu'il savait marcher sur deux pieds et rouler sur deux roues. (p. 80)

> Mais Phil et Vinca connaissaient la marée d'août et son tonnerre monotone, la marée de septembre et ses cheveux blancs échevelés. (p. 57)

Their relationship is indissociable from its context; the wild, open landscape offers a more private shelter for their intimacies than the house which they share with the adults:

> Aucun d'eux n'avait jamais songé qu'un secret pût être confié à des tentures de cretonne claire... (p. 152)

> —Comme c'est facile de vivre, la nuit. Mais pas dans les chambres. (p. 180)

Despite all this and the natural details and analogies which occur on virtually every page of the text, their natural idyll, like their childhood, is under threat: 'Le bain quotidien, joie silencieuse et complète, rendait à leur âge difficile la paix et l'enfance, toutes deux en péril' (p. 37). Even in Chapter Two, the adult world is intruding upon their natural pleasures, as Vinca is obliged, for the sake of etiquette, to abandon her swim and dress for lunch with her father's business associate (p. 38).

Vinca's perception of her natural surroundings nevertheless remains much more acute than Phil's as the novel progresses.Despite the tension of her dramatic confrontation with him in the sixteenth chapter, she remains alert to the changes and activities taking place in her environment:

> Et cependant, elle surveillait, d'un œil agile, les abords de la villa lointaine; elle mesurait en marin la chute du soleil: 'Il est plus de six heures...' (p. 165)

The same alertness proves to be deeply shocking to Phil, whose senses have been dulled by other preoccupations and in particular by his liaison with Madame Dalleray:

> —Pendant que nous étions à nous disputer, tu n'entendais pas le battement des deux fléaux. Moi, je l'entendais. [...]

> —Elle, elle l'entendait... Elle était forcenée, elle m'a frappé au visage, elle m'a dit des paroles sans suite; —mais elle entendait le battement des deux fléaux... (p. 181)

Madame Dalleray has introduced him to a decadent world in which the senses are both overwhelmed and adulterated by a taste for luxury, for objects and textures which satiate the senses (pp. 149-50). On his first visit to Madame Dalleray's house, his senses are assaulted by this luxury to the point where he loses his basic powers of orientation. By Chapter Eleven (i.e. after his seduction), his response to natural phenomena has been deadened by the more recently-remembered sensuous experiences he has undergone:

> Il ajouta, rituellement: 'Le vent a tourné, on entend l'horloge de l'église, c'est changement de temps...' et le son de la phrase familière lui parvint de très loin, d'une vie révolue... (pp. 102-103)

The tiredness induced by his nocturnal visits reduces drastically the pleasure of the activities he has always shared with Vinca—'Philippe, pâle, luttait contre son frisson et nageait les dents serrées' (p. 110). It renders him hypersensitive to the cruelty involved in their fishing expeditions and turns nature into an aggressor:

> Le palpitant sommeil de Philippe souffrit de leurs [chardonnerets] cris légers, et son demi-songe les muait en petits copeaux de métal roulé, arrachés aux casque douloureux qui coiffait son crâne. (p. 108)

> Il endurait mal le soleil reflété dans les flaques et glissait comme un novice sur les chevelures gluantes des zostères. (p. 113)

The extent of his alienation from nature is measured by his physical disorientation among familiar things, as Vinca brings him from the house to the spot where they make love. Excess has impaired the acuity of his senses and he seems to have lost all his familiar coordinates, while Vinca leads him confidently like a blind man around the various obstacles which bar his way. In his liaison with Madame Dalleray, he has been given access to a whole new world of sensual experiences, but that privilege has cost him dearly—in acquiring worldly knowledge he has lost much of his knowledge of nature.

*****

The theme of adolescence is handled with both sensitivity and lucidity in *Le Blé en herbe*. The lost Eden of childhood is a theme which recurs in Colette, invariably colouring unfavourably the world of adulthood. But Colette's romanticism must always compete with her fiercely realistic analytical propensity. Even as she bemoans the loss of innocence and freedom, her intellect and probing eye are fascinated by the process by which that loss is brought about, experienced, and ultimately accommodated.

Chapter Three

Human Relations

As we saw in our introduction, Colette was at pains to stress that the implications of her study of human relations in *Le Blé en herbe* were not restricted to the adolescent phase. Her concern to establish this point in the text itself is borne out by the frequency of her generalising comparisons and axiomatic statements which take the adult as their point of reference. Thus for every analogy which reminds us of the youthfulness of the protagonists we find several which draw attention to the archetypal nature of their behaviour, or to the emergence in them of adult behavioural patterns:

> Un peu de l'aménité des maris infidèles se glissait en lui et le rendait suspect. (p. 97)

> Elle ferma les yeux, renversa la tête [...] et ressembla, avec une fidélité étrange, à toutes les femmes qui renversent le col et ferment les yeux sous un excès de bonheur. (p. 157)

> Vinca rit, d'un rire saccadé et déplaisant, comme n'importe quelle femme blessée. (p. 158)

> Il méconnaissait, hargneux, la mission de durer, dévolue à toutes les espèces femelles... (p. 163)

> Elle accepta de le bercer, selon ce rythme qui balance, bras refermés et genoux joints, toutes les créatures féminines de toute la terre. (p. 165)

> ... cette manière femelle de révérer les lares anciens et modestes... (p. 49)

The protagonists are not simply adolescents, located firmly in time and space: they are both adults in the making and representatives of eternal male and female principles. The representative status of these characters allows

Colette to explore through them a number of fundamental questions relating to human relationships in general, notably the relationship between the Self and the Other, the nature of love, and the complexity of sexuality.

The Self and the Other

The highly complex and precarious relationship between the Self and the Other is one of the themes which has dominated twentieth-century French literature from Proust to Nathalie Sarraute. In his brief but excellent *Lecture de Proust*, in which he devotes a substantial chapter to this question, Gaëtan Picon sums up the relationship between 'le moi et l'autre' in Proust in terms of two quotations from *A la Recherche du temps perdu* which could be applied equally to the work of Colette:

> 'L'homme est l'être qui ne peut sortir de soi, qui ne connaît les autres qu'en soi et, en disant le contraire, ment.' Cette formule résume l'expérience qui s'est ouverte sur l'espoir d'une communication: 'Car on ne pense pas à soi, on ne pense qu'à sortir de soi...' Entre ces deux phrases, il y a toute l'histoire du livre.[1]

Proust's own admiration for Colette was no doubt in part due to this thematic overlap. Despite their many obvious differences, both were fascinated by the interdependence of the notions of Self and Other, by the projection of the Self and its desires on to the Other, by the desire to know and the impossibility of knowing the Other. The brevity of Colette's works precludes the sustained analysis of these questions which we find in *A la Recherche du temps perdu,* but she nevertheless returns to them and approaches them from different angles in virtually all of her novels.

In *Le Blé en herbe,* Colette has chosen a phase in the development of the individual in which the differences between the Self and the Other demand conscious recognition and a reassessment of previous assumptions about relationships. Thus, in Chapter Sixteen, Phil acknowledges with sadness that adolescence is in the process of fracturing irrevocably the integral unit formed by himself and Vinca:

> —Vinca et moi, un être juste assez double pour être deux fois
> plus heureux qu'un seul, un être qui fut Phil-et-Vinca va mourir
> ici, cette année. (p. 135)

Adolescence, with its new desires and experiences, has introduced into their
relationship the element of *soupçon* or *méfiance* which Sarraute attributes to
all human relationships. In the course of this summer, communication
between Phil and Vinca has become a minefield littered with abortive
gestures, evasive glances, misunderstandings, and newly-developed
inhibitions:

> Philippe ne soutint pas longtemps le regard de Vinca, dont
> l'azur assombri ne contenait aucun reproche. (p. 96)

> Philippe se retint de prendre le bras de son amie, et s'épouvanta
> de sa discrétion. (p. 117)

> Elle interrompait leurs causeries par un silence aussi impérieux
> qu'un bond... (p. 96)

In such passages, Phil and Vinca are forced to face the obvious but very
painful facts that their unity was an illusion nurtured by childhood proximity
and that they are separate entities whose impulses and desires are no longer
synchronised. As the assumption of similarity gives way to the awareness
of difference, their interaction becomes at one more subtle and much more
difficult.

The self-evidence of this fact does not make it any the more assimilable.
Personal identity is a precarious entity; the Self knows no absolute stability;
it is constantly seeking to transcend its own bounds, bounds which are in
the first place determined by other people, by other people's perceptions.
Thus it is vain that Phil protests his right to his own identity: '...je peux
bien revendiquer le droit d'être moi-même...' (p. 139). The 'regard' of
Madame Dalleray has already changed his perception of himself, turned him
into a man (pp. 52, 53). Even his dreams are no longer his own—in them,
his desire to recoil into his childish shell is foiled by both Vinca and
Madame Dalleray and their perception of him: 'Mais ni Camille Dalleray, ni
Vinca, dans son rêve, ne voulaient se souvenir que Philippe n'était qu'un
petit garçon tendre...' (pp. 175-6).

27

However, Vinca and Madame Dalleray themselves face similar problems in their relationships with him. Vinca's perception of herself is inextricably bound up with Phil's opinion of her—her desire for his approval transforms her customary carefree arrogance into a silent supplication:

> Le petit masque mouillé et hâlé, les yeux de la Pervenche exprimèrent tout de suite l'angoisse, la supplication, un revêche désir d'être approuvée. (p. 38)

Worse than his disapproval is his unseeing negligence which denies Vinca anything more than a shadowy existence: 'Déjà il a une manière funeste de regarder son amie fixement, sans la voir, comme si Vinca était transparente, fluide, négligeable...' (p. 33). When Vinca seeks to see herself reflected in Phil's eyes, she comes up against the reflection of another woman which challenges her status in his life:

> —Mais ses yeux bruns, trop doux, et leur blanc bleu pâle, ah! comme je vois qu'une femme s'y est mirée... (p. 167)

What Vinca fails to realise is that the other woman in Phil's life scarcely fares any better. Despite her status as a free, independent and apparently self-sufficient woman—a type which recurs in Colette's work—, beneath the surface she is as vulnerable and as dependent on the Other as anyone else. Her worldly experience allows her to cover this dependence with a show of indifference which seeks to reduce or obliterate her partner:

> Sans détourner son regard de l'étendue où couvait l'orage, elle posa de nouveau sa main sur celle de Philippe qu'elle serra, indifférente à lui et pour son seul plaisir égoïste. (p. 125)

> Elle [...] se leva nonchalamment pour aller à la baie ouverte, comme si elle oubliait la présence de Phil. (p. 127)

However, like the other characters, she is propelled by a need for recognition by the Other which takes her beyond the bounds of safety and pushes her to demand of him a declaration of love. Phil's evasiveness and confusion reveal to her the limits of her control over him and the precariousness of her role. She is interchangeable with any number of women who could have seduced him: 'Il n'a appris de moi que le plus facile' (p. 128). It is at this point that her survival instincts take over. Deflecting his gaze, she sweeps him off into a domain where oblivion blots out the awareness of one's own limits:

> Philippe la regardait approcher avidement. Elle lui mit ses bras sur les épaules, et d'une poussée un peu brutale fit chavirer, sur son bras nu, la tête brune. (p. 128)

But she has let her mask of imperviousness slip, and ultimately her only recourse is to flee the situation and the partner who has become a threat.

The desire to possess and to control is but an adulterated form of the desire to know which propels the Self towards the Other. Familiarity, such as that of Phil and Vinca, is far removed from knowledge, and often breeds assumptions and misconceptions which are ultimately challenged. Phil naively hangs on to his childhood memories in his desire to bolster his sense of power over Vinca. He fills the gaps in his contact with her with remembered scenes which reassure him of her innocence and her oblivion to his current activities:

> Elle devait dormir, tournée un peu de côté, la figure sur son bras, [...] ses cheveux égaux ouverts en éventail de la nuque à la joue. (p. 102)

After they make love, it is to the code of hearsay and axiom that he resorts for his "knowledge":

> —Mais elle, est-ce qu'elle dort ? On assure qu'elles pleurent après. Peut-être que Vinca pleure à présent. C'est maintenant qu'il faudrait qu'elle se reposât sur mon bras... (p. 184)

In persisting in his illusion of control, Phil is wilfully forgetting previous conversations which should have alerted him to the ultimate inaccessibility of the Other—conversations which all revolved around words such as 'comprendre', 'savoir' and 'connaître'. He himself was prepared to accuse both Vinca and Madame Dalleray of an inability to understand (pp. 42, 123). Despite his own rash accusations, he has been ill prepared for counter-accusations made by the person whom he thought he knew best:

—C'est si peu toi, ce genre-là !...
[.....]
—Si peu moi ?... Si peu moi ?... Voilà pourtant une chose que
tu ne sais pas, Phil, toi qui sais tant de choses. (p. 172)

—Phil, tu ne me connais pas. (p. 181)

Earlier in the chapter, he had been forced to acknowledge the "strangeness"
of Vinca and his own misinterpretation of the situation:

—Je n'ai donc jamais su ce qu'elle pensait? songea Philippe.
Toutes ses paroles sont aussi surprenantes que cette force que je
lui ai vue souvent, quand elle nage... (p. 160)

All through this crucial summer, then, he has failed not only to
recognise important signals but also to accept and assimilate explicit
challenges to his assumption of superior knowledge. His wilful blindness
leaves him hardly equipped to face his final disillusionment. He, like
Madame Dalleray, has to recognize that physical possession does not afford
the knowledge of the Other that is promised and, paradoxically, may
challenge rather than reaffirm the Self's sense of power. Phil's initial
reaction is to resort to wildly romantic and mock-heroic schemes which, he
hopes, will make Vinca notice his presence and acknowledge his recent role
in her life:

—Que je paraisse à la fenêtre voisine, que j'enjambe la
balustrade pour la rejoindre et elle me jettera ses bras au cou...
(p. 187)

However, this plan fizzles out almost immediately:

—Ni héros, ni bourreau... Un peu de douleur, un peu de
plaisir... Je ne lui aurai donné que cela... que cela... (p. 188).

It is a realisation that echoes the wistful remark made by Madame Dalleray
earlier:

—Il n'a appris de moi que le plus facile... (p. 128)

Ultimately, both are forced to recognize the limits of egocentrism.

Love

The central theme of *Le Blé en herbe* is, according to Colette, 'l'amour'. The word itself appears on numerous occasions in the course of the novel in the protagonists' deliberations, their conversations, and in the narratorial commentary. It is the focal point of the characters' attention. Notwithstanding its prominence, it remains a vague, ill-defined concept. In their use of the term 'amour', the central characters show considerable confusion and equivocation. The attempt to establish a one-to-one correlation between the word and their own experience invariably fails. Phil, Vinca and Madame Dalleray all use it as a point of reference in their attempts to define their relationship, but again and again they are forced to recognise its inappropriateness:

> L'aime-t-il donc à ce point? Il s'interrogea, ne trouva pas d'autre mot que le mot amour, et rejeta rageusement ses cheveux hors de son front.
> —Ce n'est peut-être pas que je l'aime tant que ça, mais elle est à moi !' Voilà ! (pp. 59-60)

> —Tu ne m'aimes pas assez, Phil, tu ne m'aimes pas assez ! (p. 64)

> —Vous m'aimez? dit-elle à voix basse.
> [.....]
> —Un homme m'eût dit 'oui', songeait-elle. Mais cet enfant, si j'insiste, va pleurer et me crier dans ses larmes, à travers des baisers, qu'il ne m'aime pas. (p. 127)

None of the characters can content themselves with the fluid relationships they have with each other. They must always measure that relationship against an absolute standard. 'L'amour' is at once an obsessive and an elusive goal. It is in the study of this area that Colette shows best, perhaps, her understanding of human psychology. Her view of love is ironical; it is not unkind. She acknowledges and respects its force, while illustrating the gap between ideal and reality. It is this gap which is the source of much of her irony. The ironic repetition of the word 'amour' in the following, circuitous narratorial commentary conveys not only the power of the concept, but also the confusion surrounding it and the way in which its introduction contaminates existing relationships:

> Sa tendre et exclusive camaraderie avec Phil l'avait formée aux jeux garçonniers, à une rivalité sportive qui ne cédait pas encore devant l'amour, né cependant en même temps qu'elle. Malgré la force, chaque jour monstrueusement accrue, qui chassait hors d'eux peu à peu la confiance, la douceur, malgré l'amour qui changeait l'essence de leur tendresse comme l'eau colorée qu'elles boivent change la couleur des roses, ils oubliaient quelquefois leur amour. (pp. 95-6)

The main reason why 'l'amour' proves to be such a difficult term to handle is that it eludes definition. In real terms, it is by and large a peg on to which the characters hang a multitude of other, more easily identifiable but often contradictory, emotions and desires. Furthermore, the emotions which the characters feel are not constant but are a precarious product of circumstances and events, and are subject to the unstable influences which determine the Self's relationship with the Other.

'L'amour' in Colette is indissociable from the desire to control the Other. Phil, Vinca and Madame Dalleray all desire to own the object of their affection (pp. 33, 98, 166). In placing these characters in an archetypal amorous triangle, Colette has deliberately chosen a situation in which the perversity and frustrations of human relationships can be most accurately observed. The features which attracted Phil to Vinca as a 'camarade'—her independence and rebellious spirit—constitute a threat to him as a lover; yet any concession on Vinca's part, any sign of submissiveness dampen his desire for her (p. 49). Throughout his affair with Madame Dalleray he wishes both to preserve Vinca's innocence and ignorance and to cause her the distress of having a rival which will confirm his power over her:

> —Je devrais me réjouir, pensait-il. Elle ne se doute de rien. Mais en même temps il souffrait de cette sérénité inexorable, et exigeait au fond de lui-même que Vinca fût tremblante comme une graminée... (p. 112)

The physical consummation of his relationships with Madame Dalleray and Vinca brings him little joy and much confusion, because it is the knowledge that possession is possible rather than possession itself that brings most satisfaction. The shrimp-fishing scene in Chapter One, in which Phil savours the knowledge of his ability to catch his prey yet hesitates to do so, encapsulates in symbolic terms a crucial dimension of the male's attitude to the female:

> —Vite, Phil, vite, relève le filet!... Oh! elle est partie! Pourquoi l'as-tu laissée partir ?
> Phil respira, laissa tomber sur son amie un regard où l'orgueil, étonné, méprisait un peu sa victoire; il délivra le bras mince, qui ne réclamait point sa liberté, et brouillant, à coups de havenet, toute la flaque claire:
> —Oh! elle reviendra... Il n'y a qu'à attendre... (p. 36)

The female's choices are equally frustrating. The archetypal submissive role destroys her autonomy, while independence denies the need for human comfort and real intimacy. Madame Dalleray, the older, more experienced woman has chosen the latter path. Her choice of an adolescent as a lover is symptomatic of her instinct for self-preservation. In order to maintain her own position, she must reduce that of her partner, make of him a willing slave; as Philippe thinks of her somewhat bitterly :

> ... celle-là ne savait qu'ordonner, et conduire avec une dureté dissimulée celui qu'elle élevait au rang du mendiant et d'affamé. (p. 97)

But control is a precarious asset, and the preservation of territory is a constant battle which induces the very emotion most likely to threaten that sense of control: jealousy. Throughout her relationship with Phil, Madame Dalleray is aware of the presence and status of Vinca in his life and cannot resist the temptation of jealous curiosity. Furthermore, the desire for control is fundamentally a corruption of a very basic but ever-frustrated need for certainty, and the individual is driven mercilessly to measure the limits of his or her power—a psychological mechanism which ultimately exposes the illusory nature of control and the tenuousness of the master-slave relationship. When Madame Dalleray demands of Phil a declaration of love, she is testing the limits of her power over him, and in doing so inevitably breaks the spell. Her defeat and sudden departure only highlight the price she has to pay for her autonomy. She is condemned to figure only ephemerally in the lives of her partners. It is partly for this reason that we learn so little about her in the novel. Socially she is an itinerant who preserves her freedom, but at the cost of integration.

Vinca's youth and her sheltered upbringing have preserved her as yet from the cynicism of Madame Dalleray's life style. She is still learning the rules of the game. The only role model to which she has access is that of her mother, who has opted for subservience and concession to the practical needs of the male. In her assumption of domestic chores Vinca is clearly following in her mother's footsteps. Furthermore, in her sour remarks to Phil regarding his neglect, she is beginning to sound more like a reproachful wife than an amorous young woman:

> [Vinca] l'enveloppa d'un regard de femme sagace, mûrie dans les calculs et les concessions du grand amour:
> —Pendant que tu me tourmentes, dit-elle, au moins tu es là...
> (p. 134)

The pathos of the submissive woman is only accentuated by the naivety and absurdity of youth:

> —Tu en battras une autre avant moi. Moi, je ne serai la première en rien! (p. 160)

But deep down, the submissive young girl is no less interested in control than the "independent" woman. That her territory is paltry does not deter her. Vinca is discouraged by what life has offered her mother:

> Vinca fit un effort pour évoquer un temps où sa mère, jeune fille, souffrit peut-être d'amour et de silence. Elle lui vit des cheveux précocement blancs, un pince-nez d'or, et cette maigreur, qui faisait de Mme Ferret une femme si distinguée...
> (p. 78).

She is also aware of Phil's shortcomings. Yet she clings desperately to what she considers rightfully hers with 'la constance sans repos ni scrupules qui préserve l'amante et l'attache à son amant et à la vie, dès qu'elle s'est découvert une rivale'(p. 168). In the face of defeat, her desire for control is simply channelled into fantasy:

—L'attacher, comme la chèvre noire, au bout de deux mètres de corde... L'enfermer dans une chambre, dans ma chambre... Vivre dans un pays où il n'y aurait pas d'autre femme que moi... Ou bien que je sois tellement belle, tellement belle... Ou bien qu'il soit juste assez malade pour que je le soigne...
(p. 166)

The similarities and differences between Vinca and Madame Dalleray are to be observed in their reactions to defeat. Madame Dalleray has the possibility of simply moving on, but then again there is little else for her to do. Vinca does not have that option, but she is still young enough to retreat into a childish world of fantasy. At the end of the novel, it seems that Vinca has fared rather better than any of the others. However, her insouciance and joy hinge upon the fact that the door to childhood has not yet been closed, and the consequences of her steps into adulthood are not yet apparent. Phil cannot see beyond her immediate reaction and remarks peevishly:

—Elle chante. Elle sera jolie au déjeuner. Elle criera: 'Lisette, pince-le au sang!' Ni grand bien, ni grand mal... la voilà indemne... (p. 187)

The narratorial commentary, however, adds a rider which glosses ominously her apparent evasion of damage:

De la fenêtre vide venait un fredon faible et heureux, qui ne le toucha pas. Il ne songea pas non plus que dans quelques semaines l'enfant qui chantait pouvait pleurer, effarée, condamnée, à la même fenêtre. (p. 188)

The reference to Vinca humming to herself echoes an analogy which occurs much earlier in the text when she is compared to a busy bee:

Vinca haussa les épaules et reprit sa besogne, en se parlant à elle-même tout bas comme font les vraies ouvrières, qui mènent un petit fredon humble d'abeilles occupées. (p. 131)

In the earlier passage, Vinca's diligent domestic activity, like her monologue, constituted a barrier between her and Phil. At that stage, however, the summer was not yet over and her hyperactivity, like that of the bee, was an indication of the working of natural forces. The later 'fredon' issuing from her own lips is ambiguous. It may signal a return to the domestic routine which so infuriated Phil. On the other hand it may, given the associations of the earlier analogy, be more portentous. The life of the bee, like that of the mayfly or the butterfly, has long been a symbol of ephemerality and fragility. Interestingly, Valéry Larbaud uses a similar analogy in his 'Devoirs de vacances', contained in a collection of short stories published in 1918 that suggest the transitory nature of childhood:

> Voici que le Temps nous a ramené au lieu dont il nous a fait sortir. C'est bien. Sa lenteur et sa régularité ont leurs avantages, et on peut se fier à lui. Et pourtant, une idée... S'il se détraquait tout à coup, comme lorsque le ressort d'une montre se casse et que les aiguilles se mettent à tourner si vite qu'on cesse de les voir. Alors, sans doute, on verrait les montagnes fondre comme les pains de sucre à la pluie et la vie des hommes serait aussi courte que celle des abeilles. [2]

At the end of *Le Blé en herbe* the days of this last summer of childhood are numbered. Vinca could be taken to resemble a happy, but weak bumblebee, on the threshold of a cold, autumnal world.

Sexuality

The suspension of the serialisation of *Le Blé en herbe* over its sexual content seems scarcely comprehensible to the modern reader, who is much more likely to be struck by the discretion and modesty of the text. Certainly Colette's prose is highly sensual. In her notation of the physical appearance of Vinca and Phil, Colette draws frequently upon the rich repertoire of oblique natural imagery that has been used though the centuries:

> ... sa bouche fraîche, toujours un peu fendillée comme un fruit mordu par l'ardeur du jour. (p. 61)

However, it is in her evocation of Madame Dalleray and her environment that the most suggestive passages occur. The description of the ara which she keeps as a pet is perhaps the most erotic passage in the text:

> Un ara rouge et bleu, sur son perchoir, ouvrit son aile avec un

bruit d'éventail, pour montrer son aisselle couleur de chair
émue... (pp. 83-4)

Notwithstanding the sensual connotations of such passages, however, Colette always stops short of explicit description of the sexual act.The critic André Billy, commenting on *Le Blé en herbe* shortly after its publication, expressed his admiration for the great tact with which Colette evoked the relationship between Phil and Madame Dalleray: 'la conjonction assez scabreuse de cette maturité experte et protectrice avec les seize ans maladroits et farauds de Phil.' [3] In fact, Phil's seduction by Madame Dalleray occurs in the space between two chapters, while the physical consummation of his relationship with Vinca is described in terms which stress the paradoxical nature of the experience: the conflict between scruple and desire in Phil, and in Vinca, both submission and instinctive rebellion:

> Il trouva alors la force de la nommer 'Vinca chérie' avec un accent humble qui la suppliait en même temps de favoriser et d'oublier ce qu'il essayait d'obtenir d'elle. [...] Il entendit la courte plainte révoltée, perçut la ruade involontaire, mais le corps qu'il offensait ne se déroba pas, et refusa toute clémence. (p. 183)

The explicit sexual discussion and fantasy which are so characteristic of more recent adolescent fiction is absent from *Le Blé en herbe*. [4] Even as he approaches his sexual initiation, Phil is unable to formulate with precision the nature of his desire or give a label to it:

> Il soupira, sincèrement indécis, pris, dès l'entrée à *Ker-Anna,* d'une sorte de soif, et d'une sensibilité aux odeurs comestibles qui eût ressemblé à l'appétit si une anxiété sans nom n'eût en même temps serré sa gorge. (pp. 98-9)

One of the reasons for the publisher's discomfort with the serial was no doubt the liberties which Colette was taking with archetypal sexual roles. He certainly found offensive the idea of sexual intercourse involving, and indeed instigated by, an adolescent girl. The critical reaction showed less concern for the moral implications of Vinca's behaviour, but revealed reservations relating to verisimilitude. To quote Billy once more: 'J'aime moins que Vinca se donne à Phil, encore que le scène soit bien jolie; j'ai trop l'impression que c'est "pour finir" et que, dans la vie, Vinca, qui n'a que quinze ans, souvenons-nous-en, ne se donnerait pas comme ça.' [5] It is highly significant and typical of Colette's work as a whole that in *Le Blé en herbe* it is the two female characters who engineer the sexual encounter. As Marcelle Biolley-Godino points out, Colette was one of the few authors of her time to acknowledge the sexuality of the woman:

> On ne trouve plus en effet chez Colette l'idée d'une défaite des femmes en face de l'amour physique. Leur 'don' a cessé d'être considérée comme une chute... Or elles aiment l'approche physique de l'homme, ce qui minimise son triomphe à lui. [6]

Indicative of this valorisation of female sexuality is the close attention which both Vinca and Madame Dalleray pay to Phil's body. Both female characters observe and admire the adolescent's naked torso:

> —D'ailleurs, tu es beaucoup mieux, décolleté. (p. 38)

> Par politesse, Philippe se leva, s'approcha, et ne rougit que quand il fut debout, en sentant sur son torse nu le vent rafraîchi et le regard de la dame en blanc... (p. 52)

> Elle s'appuyait sur ses bras croisés, [...] et le toisait de la tête aux pieds, comme la première fois.
> —Monsieur, interrogea-t-elle gravement, est-ce par vœu, ou par inclination, que vous ne portez pas de vêtements, ou si peu? (p. 81)

On their carefree picnic with Lisette, Vinca contributes to Phil's satisfaction with his physique by her admiring gaze:

> Vinca, debout, [...] laissa tomber sur lui le rayon bleu de son regard. Il ne bougea pas, cachant le plaisir qu'il ressentait lorsque son amie l'admirait. (p. 70)

Similarly, Madame Dalleray's eyes are drawn back repeatedly to his lips:

> Sa lèvre noircissait chaque jour et la poussée du premier poil, duveteux et fin, [...] enflait un peu sa bouche et l'enfiévrait comme la bouche d'un enfant chagrin. C'est à cette bouche que venait et revenait impénétrable, presque vindicatif, le regard de Camille Dalleray. (p. 138)

In Colette, the female characters consider their partners in the way that men are traditionally supposed to consider women, paying what, for the mores of the period, is an unusual attention to their physique.

However, Colette does not stop at creating parity in the way in which the male and female characters consider each other. She, like Proust, is fascinated by the combination within the individual of both male and female dimensions. In *Le Blé en herbe,* as in *A la Recherche du temps perdu,* the traditional male and female roles are frequently reversed, or the characters hover androgynously between the two sexes. When Phil is confronted with a more experienced partner, the feminine in his psyche comes to the fore:

> ... Philippe se sentait tout à coup fatigué, penchant et faible, paralysé par une de ces crises de féminité qui saisissent un adolescent devant une femme. (p. 53)

Vinca, in her behaviour and physique, is caught between her tomboyish childhood and womanly development and instinct:

> Son vieux béret poilu ne luttait plus avec le bleu de ses yeux et, sauf ces yeux anxieux, jaloux, éloquents, elle ressemblait à un collégien déguisé pour une charade. (p. 55)

> ... il contemplait la force évidente d'un corps chaque jour féminisé, les durs genoux ciselés finement, les longs muscles des cuisses et les reins fiers. (p. 110)

Madame Dalleray, because of the conflicting demands made by her sexual needs and her desire to remain in control of the situation, has at once to cultivate a display of alluring femininity and develop an imperiousness which is conventionally associated with the male (pp. 53, 84, 91, 123, 125, 136).

******

Relationships in Colette are never simple and rarely fulfilling. They are based upon tenuous and ephemeral balances between conflicting forces in which communication is constantly inhibited by contradictory signals, reticence, and painfully-acquired defence mechanisms. The 'amour' that is so frequently on the lips of the protagonists turns out, on closer examination, to be not an absolute value but a composite emotion, drawing upon a multitude of psychological and sexual factors which are themselves subject to the vicissitudes of time, circumstance and context.

NOTES

(1)   Gaëtan Picon, *Lecture de Proust* (Paris: NRF, 1963), p. 64.

(2)   *Enfantines* (Paris: Gallimard, 1950), pp. 224-5.This title recalls irresistibly Baudelaire's reference to 'le vert paradis des amours enfantines' (*Les Fleurs du mal:* 'Mœsta et errabunda').

(3)   *L'Œuvre,* 21 August 1923, quoted in the *Notice* by Pichois and Madeleine Raaphorst-Rousseau to Colette, *Œuvres,* vol. II (Paris: Gallimard, 'Bibliothèque de la Pléiade', 1986), p. 1706.

(4)   There is, for instance, the oneiric intensity of the 'sorte de ballade des foetus mal-aimés', composed by the teenager Moussia, which closes Marie Cardinal's *La Clé sur la porte* (Paris: Le Livre de Poche, 1972), pp. 188-90.

(5)   Billy, *loc. cit.*

(6)   Marcelle Biolley-Godino, *L'Homme-Objet chez Colette* (Paris: Klincksieck, 1972), p. 62.

Chapter Four

Narrative Point of View and Style

Narrative Perspective

In her choice of a third person, privileged point of view in *Le Blé en herbe*, Colette was breaking no new ground technically. While contemporaries such as Gide and Proust were exploring the implications of relativism for narrative perspective, Colette continued, by and large, to exploit the assumptions and conventions which underpinned narrative point of view in the nineteenth-century novel. This is not to say, however, that the choice of perspective in individual works was unthinking or arbitrary.

In *Le Blé en herbe*, the narrative technique is clearly determined by the main thematic and psychological concerns of the novel. Here, the narratorial consciousness is what is conventionally and rather loosely known as "impersonal": it is not located in a specific individual and has privileged access to the thoughts of more than one character. Impersonality, however, should not be equated with objectivity or omniscience. In his seminal work *The Rhetoric of Fiction*, Wayne C. Booth has pointed out the great variations in partiality, distance and knowledge that third person narration permits.

In *Le Blé en herbe*, the narration is neither omniscient nor objective in the full senses of the words. Our access to the thoughts of the characters remains highly restricted, principally because Colette's main interest lies in the Vinca-Phil-Madame Dalleray triangle and in particular with Phil. He is her main narrative point of reference, it is his behaviour and thoughts which we follow through the novel, and our information about the other central characters is determined by his contact and encounters with them.

Selective omniscience allows the reader access to the area of the subconversation, to the layers of thought, emotion and motives which underlie our direct and often trivial communication with each other. Such a narrative stance permits the exposure of the problems, misunderstandings, and faux pas which beset human relations. It also highlights the difficulties inherent in the interpretation of gesture, glance and expression, all of which figure prominently in Colette's fiction. The choice of a dominant narrative point of reference, on the other hand, permits a close analysis of the relationship between the Self and the Other and highlights the impenetrability of the latter. Our access to the other characters is greater than Phil's, but even we do not know what will happen to Madame Dalleray after her hasty departure, nor can we predict with any certainty at the end of the novel the effect that recent events will have on Vinca. In combining access and restriction, omniscience and ignorance, Colette, like Proust, has allowed her readers access to some of the mechanisms of human nature and relationships. To have offered more than that would have been to deny one of her fundamental tenets—the belief in the Other's ultimate unknowability.

The narrative technique is an intricate mixture of showing and telling. In general, Colette prefers to show her characters in action and discussion with a minimum of narratorial evaluation or judgment. However, as in Flaubert, there are enough interventions and generalisations for the reader to gain a fairly clear idea of the "implied author"'s opinions and sympathies .The "implied author" is not to be confused with the real author. It is a product of the evidence of subjectivity and selectivity to be found in the text and the reader's correlation of such evidence. To quote Booth on this:

> As [the author] writes, he creates not simply an ideal, impersonal 'man in general' but an implied version of himself that is different from the implied authors we meet in other men's works. [...] However impersonal he may try to be, his reader will inevitably construct a picture of the official scribe who writes in this manner—and of course that official scribe will never be neutral toward all values. Our reactions to his various commitments, secret or overt, will help to determine our response to the work. [1]

The reader of *Le Blé en herbe* does not need to ascertain Colette's age at the time of the novel's publication in order to appreciate the discrepancy in age and experience between the implied author and the protagonists. Again and again in the course of the work, the childish or adolescent reaction is qualified by a narratorial rider which stresses the naivety or inexperience of the character. Such interventions vary in sympathy according to the context. Some emphasize the pathos of those whose youthfulness and unworldliness inhibit communication with the Other:

> ... un enfant de seize ans ne saurait appeler, au secours d'un délice inespéré, une autre enfant, peut-être pareillement chargée... (p. 52)

> Il n'imaginait pas qu'un plaisir mal donné, mal reçu est une œuvre perfectible. La noblesse du jeune âge l'entraînait seulement au sauvetage de ce qu'il fallait ne pas laisser périr: quinze ans de vie enchantée... (p. 185)

Even the fumbling sexual gestures of the protagonists are not exempt from a gently ironic, if discreet commentary: 'Mais la possession est un miracle laborieux' (p. 182). Other commentaries combine sympathy and lucidity in the analysis of the masochism to be found even in the child:

> ... elle était aussi triste que toutes les enfants dédaignées qui cherchèrent, dans le pire risque, une chance de souffrir un peu plus, et toujours davantage, jusqu'à la récompense... (p. 172)

> Il l'écoutait, un peu impatient, et perplexe car il cherchait, à cet instant même, les tisons et les épines éparpillés de son grand chagrin, et n'arrivait pas à les rassembler. (p. 169)

Adulthood has given the implied author an unenviable knowledge from which the protagonists are as yet protected. Hence the bitter-sweet commentary on the fierce idealism of youth, which rejects the realities which the passing of time will force it to acknowledge:

> ... car les amants de seize ans n'admettent ni le changement, ni la maladie, ni l'infidélité... (p. 67)

Also to be noted is the following wistful intervention, with its strong Proustian overtones, that laments the inability of the young to appreciate the beauty and peace of their privileged moments:

> Philippe ne sut pas se dire: 'Il est peu d'heures dans la vie où le
> corps content, les yeux récompensés et le cœur léger,
> retentissant, presque vide, reçoivent en un moment tout ce
> qu'ils peuvent contenir, et je me souviendrai de celle-ci.'(p. 52)

Elsewhere, however, in particular in her treatment of Phil, the implied author is neither so lenient nor so retrospectively understanding. Adolescent and vulnerable Phil may be, but he is also male. While the character of Phil is given a much more gentle handling than the male characters in most of Colette's other novels, his weaknesses are nevertheless explored with lucidity and in detail. We have already seen the psychological game which he plays with himself and his partners, and the solipsism and narcissism which characterise much of his behaviour. Our access to his intimate thoughts reveals him as capable of quite sophisticated doublethink and duplicity. Even in the midst of his crisis with Vinca, even after his sexual encounter with the young woman, his thoughts turn to Madame Dalleray and the possibility of continuing his affair with her:

> Il s'arracha, en pensée, à sa présence, courut à la poursuite
> d'une voiture roulant sur son nuage horizontal de poussière,
> atteignit, comme un mendiant de la route, la vitre où s'appuyait
> une tête assoupie sous son turban de voiles blancs... Il revit
> tous les détails, les cils noircis, le signe noir près de la lèvre, la
> narine palpitante et serrée, des traits qu'il n'avait jamais
> contemplés de tout près, ah! de si près... (p. 164)

> —Si, ce soir, je disparais au haut du chemin blanc, vers
> *Ker-Anna,* si je rentre seul avant l'aurore de demain, je m'en
> cacherai si bien que tu l'ignoreras... (p. 185)

The female characters themselves, in their thoughts and remarks, share some of the implied author's clearsightedness. Vinca, in particular, is capable of confounding him with sarcasm:

> ... tu te sens le roi du monde, parce que tu as seize ans, n'est-ce
> pas ? C'est le cinéma qui te fait cet effet-là? (p. 46)

> —Tu fais comme le petit garçon des Jalon, qui est enfant de
> chœur le dimanche. Il dit, pour se donner de l'importance: 'Le
> latin, ah mais, vous savez, le latin, c'est très difficile!' mais il
> ne sait pas le latin. (p. 171)

The implied author's deflationary tactics are more subtle but no less effective. The addition of a single word can change the tone of a sentence from sympathy to irony:

> Il s'endormit aussitôt; mais pour être assailli par les plus intolérables précisions du rêve, et les plus traditionnelles. (p. 175)

The juxtaposition of alternative interpretations will reveal Phil as an adulterer in the making:

> ... avec l'orgueil d'un petit garçon libertin ou le remords mélancolique d'un époux... (p. 136)

Repeatedly, commentaries on his gestures draw attention to the melodramatic stereotypes which are dictating his behaviour:

> Et il pressa, d'une main pathétique, cette place du sein où nous croyons que bat notre cœur. (p. 85)

> ... et il secoua son mal, élargit ses épaules, rejeta ses cheveux d'un mouvement fier et traditionnel, en s'adressant mentalement des objurgations qui n'eussent pas déparé un roman d'aventures pour premiers communiants. (p. 137)

However, it is in her juxtaposition of Phil's heroic pretensions and his unromantic origins and social status that the implied author shows greatest cruelty:

> La hâte de vieillir, le mépris d'un temps où le corps et l'âme fleurissent, changeaient en héros romantique cet enfant d'un petit industriel parisien. (p. 47)

> L'inconscient besoin de dédier sa tristesse et sa sagesse le tourmentait vainement, comme tous les honnêtes petits athées à qui l'éducation laïque n'a pas donné Dieu pour spectateur. (pp. 176-7)

The Romantic literature that formed part of the educational staple diet of the late nineteenth-century and early twentieth-century bourgeoisie provided the favourable and convenient pretext for behaviour which contravened the codes which that same bourgeoisie had established. *Le Blé en herbe* has no broad social message to convey, but it shows an awareness of the let-out clauses which male-dominated bourgeois society creates for itself.

Colette's choice of narrative point of view in *Le Blé en herbe* permitted her, therefore, not only to carry out a bitter-sweet analysis of adolescence but also to demythify the male through the exposure of the fallibility, sophistries and egotism of the central male character.

Narrative Point of View and Secondary Characters

In focussing on the central amorous triangle and taking Phil as the main narrative point of reference, Colette has relegated the secondary characters to an extremely marginal position. This is a fairly common procedure in fiction which attempts to recreate the exclusive worlds of childhood and adolescence, and reflects not only the gap between generations but the strength of peer-group association. In *Le Blé en herbe,* the illicit nature of the love intrigue and the need for secrecy further contribute to the creation of an intense but private world in which parents have no role.

Here the parents are reduced to the status of 'Ombres'. Phil and Vinca are highly impatient to grow up and to leave behind the indeterminacy of adolescence, thinking of the lives of their parents with arrogance and pity:

> —Comme ils sont gais! se dit Philippe. Il chercha, sur le front gris de son père, la trace d'une lumière, au moins d'une brûlure. 'Oh ! décréta-t-il superbement, le pauvre homme n'a jamais aimé... ' (p. 78)

Parental interventions are perceived as disruptive and inept intrusions. The somewhat insensitive directness with which they discuss the future of Vinca and Phil simply succeeds in irritating the young people.

Only on one occasion is a parent allowed to show any depth of character or any real concern to communicate on equal terms with his child. But even here, the clumsiness of the adult and the selfish preoccupation of the child preclude a genuine exchange. In the short, embarrassed talk that Phil has with his father (pp. 145-50), we see a dimension of the adult which has hitherto not been exposed in his social exchanges. We glimpse a melancholy which, like that of Phil and Vinca, relates to ageing and the passing of time:

> —Si tu es comme moi, ça t'ennuiera un peu plus tous les ans. Le pays, la maison. [...] Jouis de ton reste, p'tit gars. (pp. 146-7)

Unknowingly, Phil's father comes very close to some of the preoccupations of his son, but the opportunity for communication slips past as he almost immediately proceeds to talk about practical matters such as property and the bourgeois marriage:

> Mais déjà il rentrait, parlant encore, parmi les ombres, d'où un mot ambigu, un regard l'avaient extrait. (p. 147)

Of the secondary characters, only Lisette manages to impinge on the perception of Vinca and Phil without intruding. In the idyllic picnic expedition, her presence serves to defuse the tensions between Vinca and Phil and allows the latter to bypass the confusion of adolescent sexuality and to daydream whimsically about the scene before him:

> Vinca, penchée sur Lisette, soignait quelque écorchure, tirait une épine d'une petite main levée et confiante... L'image ne troubla pas le songe de Philippe, qui referma les yeux:
> —Un enfant... C'est juste, nous avons un enfant... (pp. 70-71)

She figures only intermittently, but her appearances leave a vivid image of unselfconscious childhood:

> A côté de Vinca, une petite sœur, à peu près pareille, ouvrait des yeux bleus dans un rond visage cuit, sous des cheveux blonds en chaume raide, et appuyait sur la nappe, à côté de l'assiette, des poings clos d'enfant bien élevée. (p. 39)

> Dans une chambre, la petite Lisette protesta d'une voix aiguë, puis pleura un moment. (p. 130)

> A trois cents mètres de là, sur le pré de mer, Lisette en blanc tournait comme un volubilis blanc, et ses petits bras bruns gesticulaient... (p. 169)

Lisette is privileged because she retains the brilliance and pristine qualities of childhood, which fade in adulthood into grey banality:

> Sa jeune sœur Lisette échappait encore au sort commun et brillait de couleurs nettes et véridiques. (p. 67)

This little girl, who, significantly, manages to dig up the toys that Phil and Vinca buried in the sand years before, incarnates the self-possession and insouciance that they have lost.

Style

The style of *Le Blé en herbe* falls into two broad categories: crisp, terse dialogue and dense, melodious prose which conveys the characters' perceptions of their environment or the often complex thoughts and feelings which underlie the dialogue. The broken rhythm of the book, with its alternation between direct speech and narratorial commentary, translates into formal terms the conflicting demands made on the characters: the need to communicate with a companion while preserving one's privacy, openness to the Other versus openness to the natural world.

The facile, free-flowing dialogue of Vinca and Phil's parents is a social skill which the former have yet to master. The banal chatter of adults around them contrasts sharply with their own fumbling attempts to communicate without running the risk of embarrassment and exposure. Their former childish mode of communication through command, exclamation and unselfconscious gesture still operates in those moments when they manage to lose themselves and forget their preoccupations in familiar pursuits:

> —Phil ! Viens, Phil ! C'en est rempli, de crevettes, et elles ne veulent pas se laisser prendre ! ...
> —Naturellement ! C'est que tu ne sais pas...
> —Je sais très bien, cria Vinca aigrement, seulement je n'ai pas la patience.
> Phil enfonça le havenet dans l'eau et le tint immobile.
> —Dans la fente de rocher, chuchota Vinca derrière son épaule, il y en a de belles, belles... Tu ne vois pas leurs cornes ?
> —Non. Ça n'a pas d'importance. Elles viendront bien.
> —Tu crois ça !

—Mais oui. Regarde.
Elle se pencha davantage, et ses cheveux battirent, comme une
aile courte et prisonnière, la joue de son compagnon. (p. 35)

More often than not, however, and even in these scenes, their
communication is tainted by unavowed confusions, hesitations and
resentments. Ultimately, more important than their dialogue is the
subconversation underlying it which produces tensions, misunderstandings
and inhibitions: 'Résistances ou réflexes de la conscience, elle les a fait
affleurer au cours de conversations banales des personnages, sous des lieux
communs, donnant ainsi à ses dialogues leur double sens profond de
drames intérieurs.' [2] Until Vinca's angry outburst in Chapter Sixteen, their
conversations remain inconclusive and diversionary insofar as they are
avoiding the real issues between them. This inconclusiveness is conveyed,
rather too often one may think, through the *points de suspension* which
punctuate their dialogue.

These dialogues are framed by descriptive or analytical passages in which
Colette draws upon a rich repertoire of rhetorical devices. Colette's
descriptive style is accumulative and impressionistic. It seeks to convey
through the accumulation of concrete nouns and adjectives the multiple
demands made upon the characters' senses at any one moment. Both Vinca
and Phil are extremely open to the richness and variety of the natural world
which surrounds them, and the progress of the narrative is constantly
interrupted by the notation of their sensory impressions:

> Près de sa tête il entendait dans les paniers le chuchotement
> humide d'une poignée de crevettes et le grattement intelligent
> des pinces d'un gros crabe contre le couvercle... (p. 51)

> La marée de morte-eau, endormie sous la brume au bas du pré,
> envoyait à la plage une petite vague exténuée, qui claquait
> faiblement comme un linge mouillé, de minute en minute. (p.
> 103)

In her evocation of this natural wealth Colette draws unashamedly on the
extensive knowledge of flora and fauna acquired as a keen amateur
naturalist, a knowledge which she deemed infinitely more valuable than that
offered by the academic world:

Je n'ai été que fort peu à l'école, et mes connaissances étaient aussi élémentaires que le brevet qui couronna ma carrière scolaire.
Est-ce pour cela que la soif d'apprendre ne m'a plus jamais quittée ? Apprendre non pas ce que les livres enseignent, mais ce que la vie animale ou végétale offre à tout moment de poignant... [ ]
L'heure de la fin des découvertes ne sonne jamais. Le monde m'est nouveau à mon réveil chaque matin et je ne cesserai d'éclore que pour cesser de vivre. [3]

Her multiple and highly specific references to species and plants have brought accusations of preciousness, [4] but they are not inconsistent with the intimate knowledge of their surroundings which we have already observed in Phil and Vinca, herself named after a flower, and convey something of the author's delight in the variety of natural phenomena:

Elle abaissa lentement la poche de filet dans une cavité où l'eau marine, immobile, révélait des algues, des holothuries, des 'loups', rascasses tout en tête et en nageoires, des crabes noirs à passepoils rouges et des crevettes... (p. 34)

Ils foulaient l'origan poivré et les derniers parfums du mélilot. (p. 60)

... Vinca gravit le pré de mer plein de scabieuses. (p. 38)

Phil's openness to sensation is one of the reasons why he is so overwhelmed by the new world into which Madame Dalleray introduces him. His senses are assaulted and his disarray is conveyed by an impressionistic description; this stresses his loss of physical coordination and translates his difficulty in making sense of the scene other than in terms of strong, contrasting colours and outlines:

Il heurta du pied un meuble mou, chut sur un coussin, entendit un petit rire démoniaque, venu d'une direction incertaine, et faillit pleurer d'angoisse. Un verre glacé toucha sa main. (p. 83)

... ses yeux habitués discernèrent le rouge et le blanc d'une tenture, le noir et l'or assourdi des rideaux. (*ibid.*)

His memory of his sexual initiation remains equally disjointed and partial, and dissolves into an array of vivid but fragmentary images:

> ... le remous d'un souvenir s'étirait, noir, onctueux, prélassé entre des saillies lumineuses qui se hissaient au jour et y prenaient la couleur de l'or, de la chair, l'éclat d'un œil mouillé, d'une bague ou d'un ongle... (p. 109)

The descriptive passages of the text are also marked by the use of imagery. In her evocation of the semi-wild creature that is Vinca, Colette once again exploits her familiarity with natural species in an attempt to render the character's animal-like qualities, movements and gestures. A brief selection drawn from among the many similes will convey a little of their range and graphic quality:

> Vinca se coucha sur le flot, souffla de l'eau en l'air comme un petit phoque. (p. 37)

> ... et Vinca fermait la marche, ficelée de sweater bleu et de culottes blanches, chargée de paniers comme un âne d'Afrique. (p. 68)

> Elle paraissait seulement surprise, et respirait vite, comme la biche qu'un promeneur rencontre en forêt et qui balance, émue, au lieu de gagner [le] large. (p. 96)

In her description of Phil, Colette often uses much more ambivalent images. His youthful despotism and his physical beauty prompt comparison with Latin gods and oriental princes, but the glamour of these analogies is generally qualified by signs of immaturity, petulance and adolescent effeminacy:

> ... son visage offensé de dieu latin... (p. 95)

> ... une humeur méchante de petit dieu fâché. (p. 123)

> Le jeune homme baissa les yeux sur ses pieds nus. Un vêtement lâche, de soie brodée, le déguisait en prince oriental, et l'embellissait. (p. 124)

In the narrative passages, those which record the actions of the characters and such events as there are, the most notable feature of Colette's style is perhaps the proliferation of active verbs. In *Le Blé en herbe,* apart from the two sexual initiations, little of great consequence happens; however, a great deal of activity takes place. The passages covering the playful paradise of Vinca and Phil are peppered with verbs denoting movement, action and abrupt gesture which conjure up a world of shared activities, and which contrast sharply with the static images presented of the worlds of Madame Dalleray and the children's parents:

> Son ami plongea brusquement, saisit un pied de Vinca et la tira sous la vague. Ils 'burent' ensemble et reparurent crachant, soufflant, et riant... (pp. 37-8)

> Elle détachait pour Lisette l'arête des sardines, dosait la boisson, pelait les fruits, puis se hâtait de manger, à grands coups de ses dents bien plantées. (p. 69)

> Phil se baissa vivement, saisit les deux rubans de laine blanche et les croisa sur une cheville brune, frémissante, sèche, jambe de bête fine, faite pour la course et le saut. [...] Le pied nu, chaussé de toile, glissa entre les mains qui le tenaient et franchit, comme s'il s'envolait, la tête de Phil agenouillé. (pp. 94-5)

Sentences such as these, all relatively simple in construction, are based upon the accumulation of strong principal clauses and active finite verbs.

The analytical passages, as one might expect, reveal rather more intricate sentence structure. The analysis of emotion and interpretation of behaviour generate sentences of some considerable complexity. Thus Vinca's mixture of suffering, resistance, submissiveness and fear is rendered through an elaborate syntax which conveys in formal terms the emotional labyrinth in which she finds herself:

> ... tandis que Vinca ne sait que se taire, souffrir de ce qu'elle tait, de ce qu'elle voudrait apprendre, et se raidir contre le précoce, l'impérieux instinct de tout donner, contre la crainte que Philippe, de jour en jour changé, d'heure en heure plus fort, ne rompe la frêle amarre qui le ramène, tous les ans, de juillet en octobre, au bois touffu incliné sur la mer, aux rochers chevelus de fucus noir. (pp. 32-3)

On other occasions, the lengthy, complex sentence may be used by the narrator to qualify the simple notation of a character's reaction and to analyse it with a sophistication that, for reasons of age or inexperience, is beyond the character himself:

> Il s'essayait à la révolte et à l'ingratitude. Un enfant de seize ans et demi ignore qu'un ordre impénétrable place, sur la route de ceux dont l'amour méditait de faire des amants trop pressés de vivre et impatients de mourir, de belles missionnaires lourdes d'un poids de chair qui arrête le temps, endort et contente l'esprit et conseille au corps de mûrir dans son ombre. (p. 141)

It is also in the analytical passages that Colette indulges her love of paradox. The perversities and contradictions of the human heart never cease to fascinate her, and the paradox proves to be a highly economical and arresting means of illustrating the way in which common-sense assumptions and working definitions of words are overturned when the amorous code comes into play:

> Chassé, et même banni, il n'emportait pourtant qu'une fierté d'homme... (p. 93)

> Mendiant rebelle à l'humilité... (p. 97)

> La bouche altérée et les mains tendues, le mendiant ne prenait pas figure de vaincu. (p. 98)

The oxymoron provides her with a similar source of gentle irony and permits her to deflate, through the combination of normally contradictory or incompatible words, the dramatic, heightened emotions of the characters:

> ... une expression d'agonie bienheureuse monta de sa bouche deserrée à ses yeux... (p. 123)

> Il ne savait pas encore pendant combien de temps tous les événements de sa vie devraient buter contre ce jalon, repère miraculeux et banal. (pp. 139-40)

> ... mais il voyait aux joues de Vinca, dans ses yeux, la flamme du vin mousseux et une sorte de folie prudente qui ne le rassurait pas. (p. 173)

*****

In her style, Colette has carefully tailored her effects to correspond with the varying rhythms, moods and concerns of the narrative. Her prose is an intricate blend of often poignantly suggestive dialogue, elegiac description, exuberant narrative, and lucid analysis. No one element is allowed to dominate: empathy is always qualified by ironic distance, reason and emotion are held in a delicate equilibrium.

NOTES

(1)   Wayne C. Booth, *The Rhetoric of Fiction* (Chicago: University Press, 1961), pp. 70-71.

(2)   Anne A. Ketchum, *Colette ou la naissance du jour: étude d'un malentendu*, p. 284.

(3)   'Allocution de Colette', in her *Œuvres,* vol. II, p. 1276.

(4)   Madeleine Raaphorst-Rousseau, *Colette: sa vie et son art* (Paris: Nizet, 1964), p. 270.

Conclusion

Alongside the massive tomes of Proust and Céline, there has always been a place in twentieth-century French fiction for the brief but no less serious work. *Le Blé en herbe*, in its formal economy and thematic richness, stands alongside Gide's *L'Immoraliste*, Camus's *L'Etranger* and Marguerite Duras's *Moderato cantabile*.

The title of the work alone provides an excellent illustration of Colette's ability to invest her tale with thematic reverberations through highly economical means. At a relatively late stage of production, Colette changed the title from the somewhat banal 'Le Seuil' to 'Le Blé en herbe', a title which posed a greater interpretive challenge and allowed for a greater play of connotation. The final title is taken from the old French proverb 'Il ne faut pas manger son blé en herbe', that is, not sell one's seed-corn, a recommendation of prudence and patience that may refer specifically to financial mismanagement, for instance in the case of Rabelais's scapegrace Panurge (*Le Tiers Livre*, ch. II). But the expression, though customarily negated for morally illustrative purposes, can be used to denote the psychological reality of sexual anticipation: in a part of *Le Temps retrouvé* written at very much the same time as *Le Blé en herbe*, Proust's narrator, Marcel, describes the state of bodily promiscuity existing in wartime in the darkness of bomb shelters, where the desirable 'préambule où les yeux seuls mangent le blé en herbe' is no longer feasible.

The choice of image alerts the reader from the outset to the importance of the natural world in the text which is to follow: the sexual development of Vinca and Phil will take place in the context of that natural world and is as inexorable as the natural cycle. The fact that Colette has chosen to draw upon the cultural code in her use of a proverb is also highly relevant. The experience of Phil illustrates well the dangers of sexual precocity. Even as he tries psychologically to accommodate his initial seduction, his reflections show an effort to compensate for the loss of mystery and the weariness that the fulfilment of the sexual urge has brought:

> Du moins, cette tourmente qu'il venait de traverser, il la laissait derrière lui. Il n'en rapportait avec lui qu'une fatigue de nageur, une mansuétude vague et universelle de naufragé touchant terre. (p. 104)

His youthful arrogance preserves him at this stage, however, and he finds comfort in pity for the anxieties besetting his peers. Much later, after the departure of Madame Dalleray, he comes to envy the 'normal', rather sordid access to sexual knowledge which will be the lot of those same peers. As he melodramatically assesses the way in which his sudden initiation has "blighted" his life, he simultaneously conjures up what the alternative might have been, an alternative which allowed the pursuit of other childish and adolescent activities: 'Puis ils n'y pensaient plus, puis ils y retournaient, le tout sans interrompre l'étude, les jeux, les cigares clandestins et les débats politiques ou sportifs' (p. 140).

While Phil's distress can be seen to confirm the wisdom of the old adage, it would, I think, be highly erroneous to restrict the interpretation of the title to a warning. Colette is no agony aunt: neither here nor elsewhere does she offer precepts for the avoidance of pain. The furthering of the desire for the Other may be unwise, but it is virtually irresistible. The proverb from which Colette has taken her title is but one of the many passed on by adults to the next generation that advocate 'Don't do as I do, do as I say.' The adolescent protagonists are responding to the same impulses as those who have gone before them and are acquiring the codes, defences and inhibitions which characterise adult relationships. The protagonists themselves are 'le blé en herbe'; they are the 'graine têtue' (p. 63) which somehow, against the odds, survives.

In the body of the text, the apparently simple story line and impressionistic surface are underpinned by a tight structure and an intricate network of symbol, motif and image which more than compensate for the restrictions imposed by serialisation. While *Le Blé en herbe* does not break new ground formally, it nevertheless demands of the reader alertness to its broader thematic implications and an active interpretive participation. To relegate it to the category of adolescent fiction would be to neglect many of its central preoccupations. In her account of one summer in the lives of Vinca and Phil, Colette has gone beyond the specific to consider much more general issues: notably the nature of passion, the barriers to communication which human beings themselves create, the passing of time and the losses which it involves, the social and emotional differences between the male and the female, and the complexity of sexuality. The microcosm of the specific relationship is, here as always in Colette, a point of access to the emotional and psychological mechanisms which affect us all, regardless of age. In the creation of this representative microcosm, Colette has created a richly-textured work in which a fine balance is maintained between understatement and analysis, poetry and lucidity, intimacy and generality.

Select Bibliography

Editions

Œuvres, vol. II, edited by C. Pichois & M. Raaphorst-Rousseau (Paris: Gallimard, 'Bibliothèque de la Pléiade', 1986), pp. 1183-1276, 1697-1732.

Le Blé en herbe, edited and with an introduction by Brian Stimpson. London, Hodder & Stoughton ('Textes français classiques et modernes'), 1980.

Useful Books and Articles on Colette

Beaumont, G.	*Colette par elle-même.* Paris, Seuil, 1951.
Biolley-Godino, M.	*L'Homme-Objet chez Colette.* Paris, Klincksieck, 1972.
Ketchum, A.A.	*Colette ou la naissance du jour: étude d'un malentendu.* Paris, Minard, 1968.
Marks, E.	*Colette.* New Brunswick, Rutgers University Press, 1960.
Maulnier, T.	*Introduction à Colette.* Paris, La Palme, 1954.
Offord, M.	'Colours in Colette's *Le Blé en herbe', Nottingham French Studies,* 22 (1984), 32-52.
Offord, M.	'Imagery in Colette's *Le Blé en herbe', Nottingham French Studies,* 25 (1986), 34-62.
Olken, I.T.	'Aspects of Imagery in Colette: Colour and Light', *PMLA,* 77 (1962), 140-48.
Raaphorst-Rousseau, M.	*Colette: sa vie et son art.* Paris, Nizet, 1984.
Stewart, J.H.S.	*Colette.* Boston, Twayne, 1983.